FACING CHANGE

Facing Change

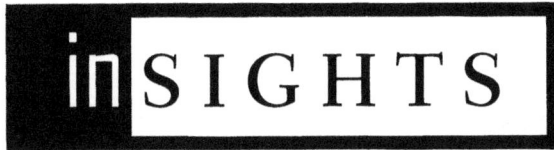

inSIGHTS

BIBLE STUDIES FOR GROWING
FAITH

LEAH MATTHEWS

WIPF & STOCK · Eugene, Oregon

Wipf and Stock Publishers
199 W 8th Ave, Suite 3
Eugene, OR 97401

Facing Change
By Matthews, Leah
Copyright©2000 Pilgrim Press
ISBN 13: 978-1-60899-222-5
Publication date 1/15/2010
Previously p ublished by Pilgrim Press, 2000

Contents

◈

USER'S GUIDE   7

PRACTICAL SUGGESTIONS FOR BIBLE STUDY   9

INTRODUCTION   11

1. JOHN 4:1–42   15

    Part I: The Encounter (John 4:1–26)   15

    Part II: Confronting the Truth (John 4:16–24)   18

    Part III: Go and Tell (John 4:25–42)   20

2. GENESIS 12:1–9—GENESIS 18:1–15; 21:1–7   23

    Part I: The Call (Genesis 12:1–9)   23

    Part II: Expectation (Genesis 18:1–15; 21:1–7)   27

3. LUKE 17:11–19
    Change through Healing   31

4. MARK 10:46–52
    A New Vision   36

5. EXODUS 15:28—EXODUS 17
    Consequences of Change   40

NOTES   45

User's Guide

◈

Facing Change is a Bible study based on biblical characters who faced change, and events requiring change, even transformation. Our world confronts us with changes every day. Sometimes the changes are small; sometimes they are monumental. Change has a lasting effect on our relationships with others and with God. This study explores how we can face change in our lives from a faith-based, biblical perspective, how God is present with us amid change, and how faith sustains us.

This study is written for adults and can be used in faith formation classes, new membership classes, seasonal study groups (Lent or Advent may be ideal), or existing Bible study groups.

This study can be completed in five to eight weeks. (The first session is divided into three parts so it can be extended to three weeks if you need the time; the second session has two parts and likewise can be extended over two weeks.)

- Be sure to have several translations of the Bible available.

- Arrange the room comfortably so people can see each other as they are talking (preferably in a circle or around a table).

Study questions are listed toward the end of each section.

Practical Suggestions
for Bible Study

One of the wonderful things about the Bible, with all its stories, is that it allows us, within certain limits, to be interpreters. It is open to you and me as we bring our own experiences to it. Bible study does not need to be boring, nor should it be. In the words of Martin Luther, "God's word has hands and feet. It runs after you. It grips you. Let it loose, then things will happen." The following suggestions might be helpful to your group:

1. Read the text from several different translations, versions, or paraphrases. Note the differences in the readings. Have several persons read the passage aloud.

2. Center yourself on the text. Get into the text by asking:

   (a) What questions, images, thoughts, or feelings does this passage evoke for me?

   (b) With what character do I identify in this passage? What is it that a particular character is saying to me?

   (c) What is the passage really saying? Don't be concerned with "did this really happen?" Rather, look more closely at what the passage means.

3. Get into the Scriptures by role-playing or creating a drama about the passage — actually be the characters.

You will discover that many of the passages can be written as plays, with or without narration. Be creative. It is not sacrilegious to explore ways to interpret the meanings of texts for us in this day and age or extract personal meaning on our own religious and spiritual journeys. Let the Bible speak to you. Do not confine your thinking to how it has always been. Contemporize the event, characters, and message as much as possible. What does it mean or what could it mean for you today?

4. Use your imagination. Many Scripture passages can be interpreted in several different ways. Try to understand the themes, and then "plug" them into your life and your faith experience. Examples: God's fairness, Jesus' inclusiveness and concern for the outcast, the lonely, the fearful.

Introduction

Change is the one thing in life that is certain. Change is a constant in our lives, and yet it is often one of the most difficult parts of life. Change is disruptive. Change causes us to break out of the ruts we sometimes enjoy. We all know disruptive changes. The workplace restructures, and suddenly you are faced with a new job. A parent or child becomes sick, and you are the primary caretaker. Some changes we create. Other changes are completely unexpected and out of our control. And yet, change also can bring new life to us, a new way of being, an introduction to a whole new way of living, a new lease on life, a new world in which to live and in which to operate. Change is at the same time scary and exciting.

The dictionary definition of "to change" is "to make radically different; to transform, to give a different course or direction, to make a shift." Change almost never comes easily. It means altering our lifestyle in some way, sometimes radically. It means leaving the familiar to face the unknown. "To transform" is defined as "to change in character or condition; to undergo a major change in form, nature, or function." In describing the differences between change and transformation, Flora Slosson Wuellner, an ordained United Church of Christ minister and profound writer on spirituality, has written:

> Change refers to adaptation, reaction, without necessarily involving any newness of being. Transfor-

mation involves much more than mere adaptation to outer manipulation. Transformation implies new being, a new creative energy flowing from the center which acts with creative power upon surrounding events.[1]

This is what is offered by God through Christ:

transformation, new creation rather than change, growing from our deep center, expanding our empowered freedom even in the midst of the power of outer events. When our inner selves waken, stretch, stand up, move out, make choices, our terror of change becomes the hunger, thirst, and ecstasy of growing.[2]

So what does the Bible have to say to us about change? Certainly there are many persons in the Bible whose stories are about change. Very often, the change comes from encounter with God. But encounter with God brings more than change. It brings transformation, and transformation means that one can never be the same again. Transformation does indeed call for "new being, a new creative energy flowing from the center which acts with creative power upon surrounding events."[3]

This study centers around persons of the Bible whose very souls were transformed by encounters with God. What do these stories have to say to us about change? How do people cope with life-transforming encounters? What is the anchor of faith in the midst of the inevitable changes in life? In pondering the meanings of the events in the lives of the persons here as you "live into" the lives of these biblical characters, seek your own meaning of those encounters with God and the transformation called forth. Find there a faith that you can embrace and that will be sustaining in the changes you may face as well.

John 4:1-42

◆

Notes for the Leader

Depending on the amount of time you have, this Bible study can be divided into more than one session. It is written in three parts for your convenience.

Be sure you have a variety of translations or versions of the Bible from which the group can read.

Make sure the room is comfortable and set up to accommodate all who will be present.

Suggestions for those who choose to do this as a drama: Make sure that you include not only the dialogue of Jesus and the woman, but also include a group representing the disciples (imagine what they are doing) and be sure to include the final verses.[4]

PART I: THE ENCOUNTER
(JOHN 4:1–26)

Jesus left Judea and was on his way back to Galilee. The route took him through Samaria and the city of Sychar, which was near the plot of ground that Jacob had given to his son Joseph. Jesus was tired, the Bible tells us, weary beyond words, and he had come to rest while the disciples went for provisions. Jesus was at Jacob's well, a geographically, historically located place. Some scholars agree that it was a large well, perhaps seven and a half feet across, perhaps nearly a hundred feet deep. And when Jesus got to the well, he was thirsty. There was a woman there, a woman who had come to fill her jar so her family could have water. Since Jesus had no way of drawing water from the well, no "skin bucket" or rope, he asked the woman for a drink.

The request seems innocent enough. But by speaking to the woman, he broke all conventions of the time, "which restricted the possibility of a conversation in a public place between a man and a woman who did not know each other, all the more if the man in this case was a teacher."[5] In talking with this woman who has come to fetch water, Jesus breaks the prohibition against talking with an outsider, someone excluded. The Samaritans were considered unclean. "How is it that you, a Jew, ask a drink of me, a woman of Samaria?" (John 4:9).

The woman was a Samaritan and Jesus initiates contact with her. He not only has conversation; he empowers the woman to see herself as she is. Her identity is reflected back to her through this remarkable conversation with Jesus the Christ. "If you knew the gift of God, and who it is that is saying to you, 'Give me a drink,' you would have asked him, and he would have given you living water." Here at the well an important conversation takes place about the living water. Living water is understood to mean running water as opposed to rainwater. Brimming water, eternal water, water as a satisfaction of a fundamental need is the way in which Jesus speaks of this water. It is very typical of the Gospel of John to refer to this common element of water with a double meaning. John intentionally uses words with a double meaning, uses the richness of language to push beyond conventional assumptions and expectations.[6] And Jesus definitely meant more than just water. The dialogue goes from the physical need of thirst for water to a spiritual longing for the water that gives life, living water. Christ's offer of water was a juxtaposition of living water with the gift of God, life-giving water. It was eternal water without limit. It was the waters of transformation for this woman who was never to be the same again.

Questions for Reflection

If the group is large, break into pairs or several groups of three or four, and ask the groups to reflect on these questions:

Have the group think about images of *living water,* their experience of water, or lack of water.

- Who or what is your well of living water?

- Where do you go to be filled?

- What is your "water hole," or place of refreshment?

- What nourishes you? What gives you life? What is your "eternal source"?

- How is this conversation about living water the beginning of change for the woman?

- How can spiritual truth bring about change for us?

PART II: CONFRONTING THE TRUTH
(JOHN 4:16–24)

"To discover Jesus is to break established patterns, to discover new realities, new worlds."[7] And that is exactly what happens to the woman at the well. The woman has come to the well at noon, in the heat of the day, maybe to avoid encounter with others of the village who came for water. She perhaps feels unworthy, the subject of the village gossip. Her encounter with Jesus is an encounter with the realities of her own life, not in a judgmental way, not as moral objection. He invites her, through their dialogue, to see the contradictions in her own life that threaten her.

There is no judgment about her life here even though we have often heard sermons judging this woman quite harshly. Jesus does not accuse her of any sinfulness. Jesus does not require any confession, is not accusatory in his conversation with her, but rather just tells it like it is. "You have had five husbands and the one you have now is not your husband" (John 4:18). There is no moral lesson to be found here except that Jesus empowers the woman to see her own life. At the well, he gave her the chance to see her possibilities, her values, her worth as a person.

"The woman answered him, 'I have no husband.' Jesus said to her, 'You are right in saying, "I have no husband"; for you have had five husbands, and the one you have now is not your husband. What you have said is true!'" (John 4:17–18). "It was as if Jesus were telling her: 'Your life consists in routines; your loves are transitory. The living water that springs from the depths, authentic faith, is built on truths. It is time to begin again.'"[8] This was a transforming moment for the woman at the well, not a quick fix but a time that allowed for a "transformation, a new creative energy flowing from the center which acts with creative power upon surrounding events."[9] This conversation with Jesus broke open her life in ways she may have thought unimaginable. It was this encounter with Christ that transformed her life, offered her the possibility that she could have a deep faith, a living faith.

Verses 19–26 follow with a discussion of religion, indicating that the woman had certainly heard of Jesus before this encounter. She said, "Messiah is coming!" and Jesus responded, "I am he!" (v. 26). "That which had surprised her earlier, that Jesus would speak to her (v. 9) appears now as a sign of the divine presence."[10]

Questions for Reflection

- At what point in this dialogue with Jesus do you think the woman began to see herself differently?

- What must it have felt like for her not to be judged but to be accepted?

- Who is the person who has turned your life around, has helped you "confront your own realities," realize your worth, and point out your possibilities? Who is the person who enabled you to transform your life so that you were never the same again? Who has believed in you when you did not believe in yourself?

- When has the truth been told to you and the reality of it caused you to be different?

- When have you been aware of a divine presence?

PART III: GO AND TELL
(JOHN 4:25–42)

The third part of the passage tells the good news. "John 4:1–42 has taken the reader on a long journey, with many interruptions in the itinerary. The text has moved us from a Samaritan woman who balks at Jesus' request for water, to the disciples who are ignorant of Jesus' food, to the Samaritan townspeople who, through the woman's testimony, open their city and their lives to Jesus."[11]

Yes, the woman has gone running — running to tell. What she has just experienced could not be contained, kept secret, held down. She left her water jar, that nourishment of life upon which her family depended, and went running. To carry the jar full of water on her head would hold her back, and she had urgent, breaking news. "Come and see a man who told me everything I have ever done! He cannot be the Messiah, can he? . . ." And many of the Samaritans from that town believed in him because of the woman's testimony: "He told me everything I have ever done" (John 4:29 and 39).

For the Samaritan woman, the meeting with Jesus was one of life's profound interruptions, when the task at hand gets put into perspective by something or someone more important. It was a moment of transformation for this woman, a moment when the ordinary, daily tasks had to be put aside to shout the good news of her encounter with Jesus.

Questions for Reflection

- What is your good news?

- Have you ever had an experience that made you leave your task at hand to proclaim the gift of new life?

- What has been a "refreshing interruption" in your life that has helped you unsaddle yourself from the water jars that hold you back and weigh you down?

- What changes did the woman make?

- What changes have you made?

- Imagine how this woman's life might be different now. Do you think she could go back to the same old routine?

- Think of those times in your life when the "same old routine" was broken and you launched out into new ventures. How did you feel? What gave you the courage to do something new?

Closing Prayer

> O God of unchangeable power,
> empower us to be prepared
> for the unexpected in our lives.
> Enable us to be thankful
> for those holy interruptions in our lives
> when new meanings break through amid old routines.
> Empower us to let go of the control
> we so much want to have.
> Give us strength and courage
> to take the risks of change.
> Ready us for your presence that may shake us
> and stir us in new ways,
> disturbing our plans,
> causing us to rearrange our calendars.
> Break into our complacency and satisfaction
> with the way things are.
> Bring new life into rituals in our lives
> that have become meaningless.
> O God of unchangeable power,
> make us willing to change. Amen.

Genesis 12:1-9—
Genesis 18:1-15; 21:1-7

◈

Notes for the Leader

There are many instances in the Bible in which God calls an individual or a community to specific tasks of ministry. The call of Abraham and Sarah is one of those occasions. Read the scripture from as many translations or versions as you have in the group. When you are finished, take a few minutes to talk about the differences in the translations and what they might mean. Have people share how they felt when they read the story. What would it be like to be Abram and be called to leave what is familiar, safe, and known? What about Sarai? (You might have the women comment on how Sarai must have felt and the men on how Abram must have felt.)

Part I: The Call
(Genesis 12:1–9)

The call of Abraham in Genesis 12 marks the beginning of unbelievable change in his life. First, there was the call of God. "Now the LORD said to Abram, 'Go from your country and your kindred and your father's house to the land that I will show you. I will make of you a great nation, and I will bless you, and make your name great, so that you will be a blessing'" (Genesis 12:1–2). Abram had

been fairly successful, a good businessman, as it were. He
had acquired many possessions and was pretty much established where he was. And off they went, Abram, his
wife, Sarai, and his brother's son, Lot. They gathered up
as many possessions as they could carry with them. On
the way they passed through the land of Canaan, where
in Shechem God appeared again to Abram and told him
he would give this land to Abram's offspring. So Abram,
being a religious man, built an altar to God there where
God's name could be invoked.

The journey was not without incident. While Abram's
business skills were good, and he seemed to be in a good
place with God, his family life left something to be desired.
As we read in Genesis 12:10–20, a little stop-off in Egypt
during the famine upset his family life a bit. So that he
could "find favor" with Pharaoh, he informed Sarai that
she was to tell the Egyptians she was really his sister. She,
of course, did what Abram told her to do, and Pharaoh,
impressed with her beauty, took her into his house as his
wife and for her sake dealt well with Abram. But a great
plague afflicted Pharaoh and his house because of Sarai,
and Pharaoh was more than annoyed with Abram for lying
to him, discovering (we're not really told how) that Sarai
was, after all, Abram's wife, not his sister. At that point,
Pharaoh made them leave Egypt.

Abram took his wife, Sarai, and "all that he had" and
Lot as well with him into the Negeb. The Bible tells us
that "Abram was very rich in livestock, in silver, and in
gold" (Genesis 13:2). Abram went to the place in between
Bethel and Ai where he had first made an altar, and there
Abram called on the name of God once again. Because Lot
was also rich, the land could not support both of them liv-

ing together. Moreover, their herders didn't get along. So Abram suggested to Lot: "Let there be no strife between you and me, and between your herders and my herders; for we are kindred. Is not the whole land before you?" Since the plain of the Jordan was fertile, Lot chose all the plain of the Jordan and they separated, Abram in the land of Canaan and Lot among the cities of the plain as far as Sodom. "God said to Abram, 'Raise your eyes now, and look from the place where you are...for all the land that you see I will give to you and to your offspring forever'" (Genesis 13:14–15). And Abram built another altar to God.

Questions for Reflection

Abram was called to leave the familiar for the unfamiliar. God didn't even say exactly where Abram was headed, but just let him know that God would be present as needed.

- Imagine for a minute the faith that Abram's decision must have taken. How would you feel if God called you to journey into the unknown? Leave the familiar? Has it happened to you? How did you deal with it?

- How do you think Sarai felt about this change? Excited? Scared? Taken for granted?

- How do you think Sarai may have experienced this whole episode?

- How does your faith in God sustain you for the changes you face in your life?

- How do you think Abram's faith in God kept him going?

- For us, life's changes — a new job, graduation, marriage, divorce, births, deaths — are events that clearly change us. How have these events changed you? For the better?

- Have they made you bitter? Or better?

PART II: EXPECTATION
(GENESIS 18:1–15; 21:1–7)

It is true that for Abram and Sarai life had changed radically. Here they were on this journey God had called them to take. However, the big problem was that Sarai had not borne any children for Abram, and therefore there were no descendants. In a conversation with God in Genesis 15, Abram said to God, "You have given me no offspring, and so a slave born in my house is to be my heir." But God reassured Abram that Abram's "very own issue" would be his heir (Genesis 15:2–4). God went so far as to tell Abram to count the stars and that indeed his descendants would be that many.

Because Sarai was feeling like a failure at this point for not conceiving and bearing children for Abram, she arranged with her slave-girl Hagar to bear children for her. "So, after Abram had lived ten years in the land of Canaan, Sarai, Abram's wife, took Hagar the Egyptian, her slave-girl, and gave her to her husband Abram as a wife" (Genesis 16:3). And Hagar conceived and was so proud of it that she "looked with contempt" on Sarai (v. 4).

Sarai didn't like Hagar's attitude and complained to Abram, who put it back onto Sarai to deal with her, and "Sarai dealt harshly with her" (v. 6). Hagar ran away, but she met an angel who told her to go back to her mistress Sarai and submit. If she would do that, the angel of God promised to multiply her offspring as well. And God went on to name the child Ishmael.

When Abram was ninety-nine years old, God appeared to him and made another covenant with him. First of all, God told him that from now on he would be called Abraham, not Abram. And his wife Sarai would from now on be named Sarah and would be blessed and bear a son. God informed Abraham that the child's name would be Isaac.

Genesis 18 tells the story of the imminent pregnancy. God appeared to Abraham by the oaks of Mamre, and when Abraham looked up he saw three men near him. He bowed to them and welcomed them, washed their feet, and told Sarah to prepare some food for them. After she did so, they asked where Sarah was. (We can assume she was in the kitchen cleaning up after their snack.) One of the visitors said, "I will surely return to you in due season, and your wife Sarah shall have a son." And Sarah was listening at the tent entrance behind him. Because Abraham and Sarah were so old, she laughed, and God said, "Is anything too wonderful for God?" God said to Abraham, "Why did Sarah laugh?" and Sarah denied doing so, for she was afraid.

If you skip on to chapter 21 you can read about the birth of Isaac. And in Genesis 21:6 we read: "And Sarah said, 'God has brought laughter for me; everyone who hears will laugh with me.'"

The story of Abraham and Sarah and the gift of Isaac is a pivotal one for biblical faith. These two old people, at an utter dead end in their lives, are promised a role in God's plans. The promise of new life, of the power of the intrusions of God, is an amazing story of faith at work. Sarah's story is one of transforming laughter — from utter unbelief to amazing belief. "Faith is not reasoned, but playful, shattering, intrusive. The parameters of the expected are broken."[12] "Is anything too wonderful for God?"

Questions for Reflection

- Hagar was a slave and was told to go to Abram. How did you feel when you read about Hagar being forced to be with Abram, forced to bear his child?

- What were your feelings when Hagar "looked with contempt" on Sarai?

- What did you feel when Sarai dealt harshly with Hagar? Did you feel sorry for Hagar or Sarai?

- What changes do you think the news of having a child meant for Sarah and Abraham?

- Did you feel God's presence with you when there have been major changes in your family? Can you describe how that felt?

- Have you ever had something happen to you that was so ridiculous all you could do was laugh?

- What impact did the birth of Isaac have on the lives of Abraham and Sarah? How were they changed?

- What can we learn about facing change from these events and the ways in which Abraham and Sarah dealt with them?

Closing Prayer

God of steadfast love, we give you thanks
for the "holy interruptions" in our lives.

When those times come to us we
are not always happy about it.
Often we are fearful of the changes they require of us.
You call us to do a new thing, O God.

It is you, O God, who open up to us
so many new possibilities.
But we fumble our way and miss the opportunities
you place before us.
Help us be attentive to your voice
and to your will for us.
Lead us into the unknown
with courage and with faith.
Fortify us with your presence.
In the name of the Christ. Amen.

Luke 17:11-19

CHANGE THROUGH HEALING

◈

Notes for the Leader

Read the story of the ten lepers and have each member of the group be one of the ten. Have each imagine what it would be like to be healed and get on with life. Have someone play the part of Jesus as healer. When you are finished, talk about how each felt isolated from the larger community and then healed and reunited. Imagine together the changes in the lives of the ten lepers and list them on newsprint.

What do you think was different about the man who returned to give thanks?

There are many Bible stories that include healing. In fact, someone has said that to take the healing stories out of the Bible would leave us with an almost empty shell. Jesus' healing stories take place in many and varied situations. Some people seek Jesus on their own; others are brought to Jesus by friends who know of his healing power.

In the New Testament biblical culture leprosy was, according to the law, a disease that made people "unclean." Leprosy was a frightening disease that would eat away at skin tissue until fingers or toes would fall off. Scarring and disfigurement were typical. People who had leprosy were social pariahs and therefore ostracized to a colony of lepers. "Leprosy" was not Hansen's disease as we know it today, but rather a very contagious disease of the skin. In fact, people were so afraid of getting it that those with leprosy were required to call out, "Unclean, unclean!" if others came near them.

When the ten persons with leprosy approached Jesus shouting, "Jesus, Master, have mercy on us!" Jesus was moved by their cries. "Again and again the Gospels subtly suggest the sensitivity of Jesus to need, to pain, to disinheritance, to lostness."[13] Jesus instructs the lepers to see a priest, and on the way they are healed. The priests in those days were the only ones who could determine whether a person was healed from leprosy; only after the decision of the priest could a healed person go back to the community.

As these ten went on their way to the priest, their bodies were healed. Nine went on their way. One returned "praising to God with a loud voice" (Luke 17:15), showing gratitude from the depths of his being. This man knew that he had just been given a second chance, a new lease on life, an opportunity to live life as a whole person. And his gratitude bubbled up from the very depths of his soul. Jesus responded, "Were not ten made clean? But the other nine, where are they? Was none of them found to return and give praise to God except this foreigner?" (Luke 17:17–18). The foreigner was in fact a Samaritan. Once again we find Jesus crossing the boundaries, breaking the rules, including all persons in the possibilities of a place in God's realm.

Not only was the foreigner the only one to return to give thanks, but he was a Samaritan, an outsider. Jesus responds to the one who gives thanks, "Go. Your faith has made you whole" (v. 19, KJV adapted). The man was so thankful for Christ's healing, so grateful to be whole again, that he came back to express his gratitude. We can be sure that this man was changed from the inside out. He was transformed. He was given a "new being, a new creative energy flowing from the center which acts with creative power upon surrounding events."[14] Jesus' act was not just a healing of the outside disease but an "unfolding from within."[15]

Martin Bell, in a little book called *The Way of the Wolf*, speaks on behalf of the other nine in a story entitled "Where Are the Nine?"[16] Bell suggests various reasons for the other nine not returning to give Jesus thanks. One was scared; one didn't believe it was Jesus who did the healing; one thought there wasn't time to give thanks before the realm of God closed in; one was just bitter; one was very pleased and then simply disappeared; one didn't really want to be healed because he wouldn't know how to live in the community as a whole person; one was in a hurry to get home; one was so thrilled, so full of joy, that he just forgot to give thanks; one thought there should be more to it than just going to the priest, that there should be some difficult times to go through, like fasting and right living. These are all reasons that we can relate to in our own lives. Changes in our lives sometimes leave us filled with thankfulness and other times fill us with anxiety and dread, confusion and uncertainty.

Questions for Reflection

- Have you ever known anyone whose life was consumed with medical problems?

- Have you ever thought that those medical problems defined that person?

- How would that person respond to being healed?

- How might life change for that person?

- How might you see that person differently?

- When something good happens to you, do you thank God or do you just take the credit for deserving it?

- How will being healed change the lives of the lepers? Imagine what it would mean for each one.

- Do you think the man who returned to give thanks was more religious than the others?

- When Jesus said, "Your faith has made you whole," what do you think he meant? Some translations say, "Your faith has made you *well.*" Is there a difference between wellness and wholeness?

- How would you define "whole" as the word is used by Jesus?

- Healing changes our whole perspective on life. Think of times in your life when you have been sick. What changed when you felt better?

- Were you thankful when you were healed spiritually, emotionally, physically, or did you just take it for granted that you would get well?

Closing Prayer

*Loving and healing God, we give you thanks
for the graceful strength of your love for us.*

*We are grateful for those times in our lives
when your healing power has touched us
and for those opportunities we have
to bring healing to others.
Sometimes a touch, a smile,
or a kind and gentle word
is all it takes.
Remind us that a cup of water,
the simple gesture,
given in your name
can make the difference in someone's day.*

*We give you thanks for the courage to face
the changes that come to us in life,
the opportunities we have placed before us.
Be with us if we panic in the face of change.*

*Give us courage to face difficult transitions
and the will to live courageously in the present.
Bless us now with your caring presence.
In the name of the Christ. Amen.*

Mark 10:46-52

A NEW VISION

◈

Notes for the Leader

Have the group read the passage about Bartimaeus, the blind beggar, from as many different translations or versions as you have available. After the reading, take a few minutes to look at the differences and talk about what they mean. Have the group share how they felt about the characters in the story. How would it feel to be Bartimaeus? The crowd trying to shut him up? How do you think it would feel to be in a situation where a crowd is depending on you for a keynote speech or sermon and one person is disruptive? How do you think Jesus must have felt?

The stories of healing very often are inserted into the text to help the reader understand the power of God, particularly through Jesus. "The miracle stories of the Gospels are the testimony of faith. They are told not so much to create faith as to testify in faith, and often in retrospect, to the mysterious power of God in this Jesus about whom they were told."[17] The story of the healing of blind Bartimaeus is a story giving testimony to faith. The ten lepers cried out, "Jesus, have mercy on us!" and so did the blind beggar. But instead of instant healing, as in the story of the ten lepers, Jesus says to Bartimaeus, "What do you want me to do for you?" (Mark 10:51). Bartimaeus responds, "My teacher, let me see again." And Jesus says, "Go; your faith has made you well" (Mark 10:51–52). The writer of Mark's Gospel then tells us that "immediately he regained his sight and followed him [Jesus] on the way" (Mark 10:52).

This is an unusual text in that it includes Jesus' words, "What do you want me to do for you?" Don't you think it would be obvious that this man was blind and would like to see? Jesus may have been testing Bartimaeus to be sure he wanted to have his sight restored. And so, with careful sensitivity, Jesus asks the question, "What do you want me to do for you?" We read that Bartimaeus was very insistent on being noticed by Jesus, crying out in a loud voice, risking ridicule from the crowd. Many told him to be quiet, but when they did so he got louder still. When Jesus heard him, he "stood still and said, 'Call him here.'" And those who had tried to quiet the man said, "Take heart; get up, he [Jesus] is calling you." And Bartimaeus threw off his cloak, sprang up, and came to Jesus (Mark 10:49–50).

The Interpreter's Bible points out the contrasts in this story. Here was a "multitude" of people and this lone individual sitting by the roadside begging (Mark 10:46). Jesus turns his attention to this one individual who cried out to him. Jesus often noticed the least and the lost. He spoke often in parables about the small things, ordinary things: water, bread, yeast, mustard seed. One blind man caught Jesus' attention and his compassion. Jesus stopped and paid attention to the needs of the man. "What do you want me to do for you?" Bartimaeus said, "Let me see again." Bartimaeus, in spite of his physical blindness, had a deep spiritual insight, a deep faith in Jesus' ability to heal through the grace of God. He had a belief that he might see again. And his sight was restored. Jesus said, "Go; your faith has made you well." Thus ends the last healing we find in Mark. "It was a roadside ministry, which could make no difference to the great end Jesus had in view."[18] But it made a huge difference in the life of one man, this blind beggar. Restored sight, a new vision, a new lease on life was the gift of God through Christ.

Questions for Reflection

A woman came to my office grieving over the loss of her son, who had been killed twenty years earlier. With a scrapbook filled with photographs of him, she said, "I just can't seem to get over his death." I suggested to her that first she must "let go" of the scrapbook; she must let go of him. She had to decide that she wanted to "get over his death." No healing, physical, emotional, or spiritual, can take place unless we decide we want healing. Bartimaeus clearly desired to have his sight restored no matter what, and he had faith it could happen.

- Have you ever held onto something painful because you just couldn't seem to let go?

- How do you think "getting over" her son's death would change the life of this woman? What risks would she be taking to get on with her life?

- Jesus may have known that restored sight for Bartimaeus would mean enormous changes. What if Bartimaeus did not want to work?

- What if he had no place to go? No family to take him in?

- We do know that he followed Jesus, so we do know he left a world familiar to him. What if his identity was based on being a beggar? How do you think he would adapt to being "back in the world"?

- There is a popular little WWJD slogan (What Would Jesus Do?). If you had the opportunity to speak directly to Jesus, how would you respond to his question, "What do you want me to do for you?"

- Once again we hear Jesus speaking the words, "Your faith has made you whole." His wholeness was more than physical healing. It was a spiritual healing as well. We are told that Bartimaeus followed Jesus on his way now to Jerusalem. What do you think his life was like as a follower of Christ?

Closing Prayer

God of love and power,
we pause to give you thanks for many blessings.

Help us to gain insight into your love for us
as we hear and interpret the story of Bartimaeus.

Restore our sight so that we might see clearly
the deep love and compassion Jesus had for all persons,
even those who were the lowliest.
Have mercy on us, O God,
as we too stop to see persons as they really are,
in all of their neediness.
Stop us in our busyness
so that we too might take time to care
for even one in need.
O God, open our eyes so that we may see
the needs of this world more clearly
and respond with love.
In the name of Christ. Amen.

Exodus 15:28—Exodus 17

CONSEQUENCES OF CHANGE

Notes for the Leader

You may want to show Disney's *Prince of Egypt* as another way of seeing the story about the sojourn in the desert. If not, simply read the story, particularly Exodus 15, 16, and 17. Our focus for this Bible study will be on what some scholars call the "murmuring motif."

If you show the movie, be sure to take some time after the showing to allow people to talk about their reactions to it. Questions to guide their reflections include:

- How did you feel while watching this?

- Did you learn anything new or was your memory refreshed about the story?

- What surprised you?

- What caused you to feel uneasy or have negative feelings?

- Could you identify with any of the characters?

- What did you think about God during this story? Was God fair? Was God faithful?

During the "wilderness sojourn," the Hebrew people were free from the bonds of Pharaoh. After the miraculous crossing of the Red Sea, Moses led the Israelite people into the desert. They had been traveling for three days. Imagine their thirst! They arrived in Marah, but the water in Marah was bitter (*Marah* in Hebrew means "bitter"). Some scholars believe that there simply wasn't any water, since it was desert, and this story developed to explain how the oasis got its name, "bitter."[19] "So the people grumbled against Moses, saying, 'What shall we drink?'" (Exodus 15:24). Moses' leadership is being tested, as is God's presence. After all, the people trust Moses to lead them to some better place than the slavery of Egypt. But dying of thirst doesn't seem much better. Moses complains to God: "Come on, God. You promised you'd take good care of us, and now you're making me look like a fool." And God shows Moses a piece of wood to throw into the water, and the water becomes sweet. "There the LORD made for them a statute and an ordinance and there God put them to the test. God said, 'If you will listen carefully to the voice of the LORD your God, and do what is right in God's sight, and give heed to God's commandments and keep all God's statutes, I will not bring upon you any of the diseases that I brought upon the Egyptians; for I am the LORD who heals you'" (Exodus 15:25b–26). It's a deal. God has restored the people's faith in Moses as leader and has also established a measure of sovereignty over the people. God is now clearly in control.

As we move to Exodus 16, the complaints are of hunger. "If only we had died by the Lord's hand in Egypt! There we sat around pots of meat and ate all the food we wanted, but you have brought us out into this desert to starve this entire assembly to death" (Exodus 16:3, NIV). Life wasn't just difficult for the Israelites in this new setting, on this new journey to freedom. They were starving, and they were sure they were going to die. "This long narrative is paradigmatic for the crisis of faith that occurs between bondage and well-being."[20] The people were saying, "This is no better than the way we had it in Egypt. In fact, Egypt was better. Even though we were slaves and in terrible bondage, even though our lives were horrible, at least we had enough to eat."

In response to the complaining, God promises to provide "manna" from heaven to be gathered one day at a time, no more, no less. "Then the LORD said to Moses, 'I am going to rain bread from heaven for you, and each day the people shall go out and gather enough for that day. In that way I will test them, whether they will follow my instruction or not. On the sixth day, when they prepare what they bring in, it will be twice as much as they gather on other days'" (Exodus 16:4–5). Enough will be provided for the Sabbath so there will be plenty to eat without gathering on the Sabbath. God heard the complaints of the people and responded.

The Israelite community set out from the Desert of Sin, traveling from place to place as the Lord commanded. They camped at Rephidim, but there was no water for the people to drink. So they quarreled with Moses and said, "Give us water to drink." Moses replied, "Why do you quarrel with me? Why do you test the LORD?" (Exodus 17:1–2). Once again the people complained to Moses, "Why did you bring us out of Egypt, to kill us and our children and livestock with thirst?" (Exodus 17:3). So Moses once again turned to God, saying, "What shall I with this people? They are almost ready to stone me!" (Exodus 17:4). You can almost hear it: "Come on, God. I've done everything you want, but you're not keeping your part of the bargain. And now these people doubt my leadership. In fact, they are about to kill me."

So once again God tells Moses what to do. "Go on ahead of the people, and take some of the elders of Israel with you; take in your hand the staff with which you struck the Nile, and go. I will be standing there in front of you on the rock at Horeb. Strike the rock, and water will come out of it, so that the people may drink" (Exodus 17:5–6a). Moses did what God told him to do, water gushed from the rock, and the place was called "Massah and Meribah," meaning "testing and quarrelling."

Questions for Reflection

- Do you think it is necessary to go through hard times for change to take place?

- Does God "test" us to see if we can follow what God wants us to do?

- Have the changes in your life ever seemed to take you to a place that was more difficult than the situation you left behind?

- Are you a complainer? What would you have been saying if you were among the thirsty people?

- Does the way in which God responds to the Israelites' complaints give insight into how God might respond to us?

- Can we count on God as we face the changes in our own lives? How do you know?

- Does God cause bad things to happen to us when we don't listen for God's voice in our lives? Why do bad things happen to good people?

Closing Prayer

> *God of our ever-changing lives,*
> *we give you thanks for the constancy*
> *of your presence with us.*
> *We trust that you hear us in our need.*
> *We trust that you are there for us*
> *when things aren't going just right.*
> *O Great Provider, help us to discern*
> *between that which we absolutely need*
> *and that which is extraneous for our living.*
> *Help us to live simply without the extra baggage*
> *that just weighs us down and holds us back*
> *from doing the things that are important.*

> *Be with us in all the changing circumstances*
> *of our lives. Amen.*

Notes

1. Flora Slosson Wuellner, "Transformation: Our Fear, Our Longing," *Weavings* 6, no. 2 (March/April 1991): 8.
2. Ibid.
3. Ibid.
4. Some of the materials in Session One were first published in *Common Lot* (Winter 1993), a publication of the Coordinating Center for Women of the United Church of Christ.
5. José Míguez Bonino and Néstor Oscar Míguez, *That You May Have Life: Encounter with Jesus in the Gospel of John* (New York: Mission Education and Cultivation Program Department for the Women's Division, General Board of Global Ministries, United Methodist Church, 1991), 18.
6. Gail O'Day, *The Word Disclosed: John's Story and Narrative Preaching* (St. Louis: CBP Press, 1987).
7. Míguez Bonino and Míguez, *That You May Have Life*, 21.
8. Ibid., 22.
9. Wuellner, "Transformation," 8.
10. Míguez Bonino and Míguez, *That You May Have Life*, 23.
11. O'Day, *The Word Disclosed*, 5.
12. William Willimon, *Pulpit Resource* (Summer 1996).
13. O. C. Edwards Jr. and Gardner C. Taylor, *Proclamation* (Minneapolis: Fortress Press, 1980), 22.
14. Wuellner, "Transformation," 8.
15. Ibid., 9.
16. Martin Bell, *The Way of the Wolf: The Gospel in New Images* (New York: Seabury Press, 1970).
17. John Rogers Jr., *Proclamation* (Minneapolis: Fortress Press, 1985), 32.
18. *The Interpreter's Bible* (Nashville: Abingdon Press, 1951), 7:822.
19. *The New Interpreter's Bible* (Nashville: Abingdon Press, 1994), 1:806.
20. Ibid., 812.

This is the second in a series of study booklets designed to explore biblical topics of interest to adults. Titles in the Insights series include:

User's Guide to the Bible

Women in the Bible

The Bible and Spiritual Disciplines

The Bible and Sexuality

The Bible and Decision-Making